The ultimate busin[...] from Bloomsb[...]

The new *Business Essentials* series fro[...] pocket guides on a wide range of busi[...] performing well in interviews, to making the most impactful presentations, finding the right work/life balance, brushing up your business writing skills, managing projects effectively, and becoming more assertive at work.

Available from all good retailers and bookshops, as well as from Bloomsbury.com

BLOOMSBURY BUSINESS

Get That Job: CVs and Resumes

How to make sure you stand out from the crowd

BLOOMSBURY BUSINESS

LONDON · OXFORD · NEW YORK · NEW DELHI · SYDNEY

BLOOMSBURY BUSINESS
Bloomsbury Publishing Plc
50 Bedford Square, London, WC1B 3DP, UK
29 Earlsfort Terrace, Dublin 2, Ireland

BLOOMSBURY, BLOOMSBURY BUSINESS and the Diana logo are trademarks
of Bloomsbury Publishing Plc

First published in Great Britain in 2004 by Bloomsbury Publishing Plc
Revised edition published in 2009 by Bloomsbury Publishing Plc
(under the A&C Black imprint)
This revised and updated edition published in 2022 by
Bloomsbury Publishing Plc

Bloomsbury Publishing Plc does not have any control over, or responsibility
for, any third-party websites referred to or in this book. All internet addresses
given in this book were correct at the time of going to press. The author and
publisher regret any inconvenience caused if addresses have changed or sites
have ceased to exist, but can accept no responsibility for any such changes

A catalogue record for this book is available from the British Library

Library of Congress Cataloguing-in-Publication data has been applied for

ISBN: 978-1-3994-0065-7; eBook: 978-1-3994-0066-4

2 4 6 8 10 9 7 5 3 1

Text design by seagulls.net

Typeset by Deanta Global Publishing Services, Chennai, India
Printed and bound in Great Britain by CPI Group (UK) Ltd, Croydon CR0 4YY

To find out more about our authors and books visit www.bloomsbury.com
and sign up for our newsletters

Contents

Assess yourself

Although CVs are only a part of the whole job-hunting process, they are normally the way you get to meet a potential employer and sell yourself face to face. This questionnaire is designed to get you thinking about your skills, and to give pointers about how to play up your strengths in your CV and covering letter.

Where you are asked to give a rating, think of 1 as the lowest grade (i.e. poor, very little) and 5 as the highest (i.e. excellent, very much).

Consider the five skills your potential employer might view as most important (if you are thinking of a specific job, the job description or advertisement should give you some ideas). Give yourself a rating for each skill.

.... 1   2   3   4   5
.... 1   2   3   4   5
.... 1   2   3   4   5
.... 1   2   3   4   5
.... 1   2   3   4   5

Rate the match between your skills and your overall career goal.

1   2   3   4   5

Choose three of the following attributes that you think best suit you:

- team player
- hard working
- intelligent
- creative
- eloquent
- friendly
- honest
- serious
- diplomatic
- reliable
- conscientious
- professional

Think how you can best introduce these in your CV or covering letter.

Make a list of any extra skills that may help you stand out from the crowd of other applicants. How would you grade yourself for each skill?

. . . . 1	2	3	4	5
. . . . 1	2	3	4	5
. . . . 1	2	3	4	5
. . . . 1	2	3	4	5
. . . . 1	2	3	4	5

Rate yourself on each of the following interpersonal skills:

Communication	1	2	3	4	5
Assertiveness	1	2	3	4	5
Diplomacy	1	2	3	4	5

| Negotiation | 1 | 2 | 3 | 4 | 5 |
| Teamwork | 1 | 2 | 3 | 4 | 5 |

It's often useful to include a list of your IT skills. For example, rate your ability for each of the following:

Word processing (e.g. Word)

    1   2   3   4   5

Spreadsheets (e.g. Excel)

    1   2   3   4   5

Databases (e.g. Access, SQL Server)

    1   2   3   4   5

Programming (e.g. HTML, Java, C++, Swift, Python)

    1   2   3   4   5

Design applications (e.g. Adobe CC: InDesign, Illustrator, Photoshop, Sketch)

    1   2   3   4   5

What is your main achievement of the past two years?

. . . .

. . . .

How could you relate this to the position you are applying for?

. . . .

. . . .

Think of the most important aspect of your education to date, and rate its usefulness to you in your job hunt.

    1   2   3   4   5

Rate the experience gained from your leisure activities.

1   2   3   4   5

If you are considering changing career, think of the three skills you possess that could be most successfully transferred to your new potential career:

. . . .

. . . .

. . . .

1
Identifying your goals and your key skills

If you've not written a résumé or CV (curriculum vitae) before or haven't updated one for a while, making a start can be daunting. It needn't be like that, though, and it is worth spending some time doing some planning before you start. Don't worry yet about how to set out all you want to say and what style of type you want to use. Think instead about your 'marketable' skills – in other words, what will make you attractive to a prospective employer.

Most of us think too narrowly about the skills we have to offer and as a result tend to undersell ourselves when we are looking for a new job or promotion. Here is a step-by-step guide to examining your life and work experiences, so that you can assess what your strengths are and 'sell' yourself more effectively on your CV.

Start by contemplating your personal and professional goals. What educational, career, and leisure experiences have you had that will help you in your future job? Do you have a realistic picture of the match between your skills and your overall career goal?

Step one:
Understand the real purpose of a CV

A winning CV is not one that gets you the job – it is one that gets you the interview and so helps you get your foot in the door. Some people think that a fantastic CV alone will secure them their dream job, but that is rarely the case. For most recruiters, advertising a job and asking for CVs acts as a preliminary 'sifting' process, whereby they can look out for the people with the right skills, experience and suitability for a given role, and then fix a time to meet them in person.

You need to create a CV that stands out from the crowd and that interests a potential employer enough for them to want to meet you in person or on a video call. The employment market's never been more competitive, and a human resources manager or recruiter can receive hundreds of CVs for every job opening. Even if you're not applying for an advertised position, but are instead hoping to register with an agency, you need to make sure that your CV looks impressive and well planned. Remember that you only have a few seconds to capture someone's attention, and you don't want it to be for the wrong reasons! All of the above may sound daunting, but don't worry: the steps outlined below will help you put together the CV that you need to make a big impact, whatever job you're after.

Step two:
Begin at the end

Your CV is your chance to advertise your most marketable skills. Preparing a list of these may seem like hard work, but it is well worth doing. This list will help you to write a more powerful CV, as well as to present yourself more professionally to a potential employer. It's also excellent preparation for an interview – you will feel confident about what you have to offer and will sell yourself better.

To best help you identify your marketable skills, you need to know what kind of a position you're looking for as it will help 'frame' your job search. This will make you focus on the skills that you will need in your next job. This is the time, then, to work out what you want to achieve in your future career.

Generally, people tend to submit speculative or targeted CVs. If you have just graduated, you are working but unhappy in your current position, or you were recently made redundant, then you are probably planning to contact a large number of potential employers in different organizations. In this case, you are conducting a general or speculative career search so you will need to use several different CV formats. For instance, if you have a background in both IT and photography, you might have one CV that highlights your photographic skills for one set of employers and another CV that highlights your IT skills for another set of employers.

If, on the other hand, you are currently working and someone contacts you about a specific job opening at another company, or perhaps you learn about an opportunity for promotion within your current company, you are doing a targeted career search, and you should custom-design your CV to fit that particular job.

Step three:
Think about your career objective

Before writing your CV, you should have a very clear idea about which job you are looking for and the kind of company you would like to work for. If you are submitting a speculative application or registering your CV with an agency, you might want to include your career objective at the top of your CV, directly after your contact details. This will help people know exactly what type of job you're looking for.

Be as specific as you can. It's not enough to say, 'Seeking a middle management position in a dynamic organization' (see below and opposite); you need to be clearer and describe your ideal job. However, make sure you don't go over the top and assign yourself a long list of impressive-sounding adjectives that are either untrue, or which you can't demonstrate in person. Be concise, clear and honest.

Draft career objective:

Position in the broadcasting industry.

This statement is too general.

Improved career objective:

An experienced broadcasting professional seeking a position that will make full use of an in-depth background as a television producer, production manager, scriptwriter and networker. I am looking for a challenging production manager position that will enable me to both use and expand my creative skills and international experience in the broadcasting industry.

Draft career objective:

Managerial position in a finance organization.

This statement is too general.

Improved career objective:

A highly motivated professional seeking a position that will fully exploit my advanced education in managerial accounting and experience in all areas of finance and cost control. I have a proven ability to define key organizational issues, propose solutions and implement changes.

Step four:
Write a brief biography

Now that you know what you are aiming for, sit down and write a detailed history of where you've been and what you've learned so far in your life. As you write about each experience, describe what you enjoyed and what you didn't enjoy, and what you accomplished. What are you most proud of? Then describe what you did when you were not working, and how you felt about those activities. Make sure that there are at least seven key events in your biography. Think about:

- significant events when you were growing up;

- educational achievements;

- important life experiences, such as travelling, raising a family, or caring for a partner or family member;

- a summary of your work experiences.

Step five:
Review your experiences

1: Education

Use these questions to work out some of your skills and interests:

- Which teachers or lecturers did you like best and why?

- Which teachers or lecturers did you like least and why?

- Which subjects did you like best and why?

- Which subjects did you like least and why?

- In which subjects did you get the best marks and why?

- In which subjects did you get the worst marks and why?

- How have you furthered your studies since leaving full-time education? What motivated you?

- If you've recently decided to gain a new qualification or take up a new educational interest, what motivated you to do that?

Take some time to think about your answers to these questions and how they might relate to your job search and your skills. For example, if you found that, on reflection, you enjoyed classes or seminars that forced you to think on your feet or present your thoughts to large groups of people, you could be the type of person to flourish in a sales role.

Whatever your findings, try to draw out five key skills, motivations or areas of knowledge that you might like to use in your next position.

2: Work

Now think about your life thus far at work. Look back at each of the jobs you've had and ask yourself:

- Which was my favourite job and why?

- Which was my least favourite job and why?

- Which of these jobs would I do even if I didn't get paid? Why?

- Which jobs really challenged me and helped me to develop personally and professionally? Why?

Now identify five key skills or knowledge areas that you might like to use in your next position.

3: Leisure

What do you really enjoy doing with your leisure time (whether this is in the evenings or weekends, or during longer periods of time between jobs)? Think about:

- What marketable skills have you developed from a hobby? For example, if you enjoy hunting in antiques markets, you may have found you've gained good negotiating or influencing skills from haggling with vendors.

- What skills have you developed from your travels? For example, have you learned a new language or worked abroad?

- What skills have you developed from other leisure activities? For example, if you play sport regularly, have you found that you enjoy leading or motivating others as captain or vice-captain of your team? Or are you more of a team player who prefers a supporting role out of the limelight?

- Is there something you do for fun that you always dreamed of getting paid for? For example, if you enjoy spending time in your garden, would you love to design other people's gardens for them?

Again, identify the five most marketable skills you've gained from your leisure activities.

4: Other areas of your life

Many people today take career breaks in order to spend time looking after or raising children, or caring for ill relatives. Some of us need a change of scene after a particularly long or stressful project and go travelling for a while, or have to bounce back after a life-changing event, such as illness, bereavement or redundancy.

Even these very stressful experiences can provide us with helpful perspectives on life so think back over things that have happened to you and see how they've shaped your life and your goals.

For example:

- If you have a family, how has raising your children changed the way you do things? Have you found that you've strengthened your organizational or time-management skills? Have your priorities changed?

- If you have been a carer for a friend or family member, what strengths in your character has that experience brought out? Have you found that you are a good listener, or that you can motivate others when they are feeling low?

- If you've undertaken voluntary work, have you gained transferable skills or qualifications from that? What did you achieve in that work environment that makes you feel proud?

5: List your achievements

Now re-read what you have written and list at least 10 major achievements in your life. It doesn't matter if they're not work related. Then rank your achievements in order, with '1' being the most important achievement and '10' being the least important.

Step six:
Put everything together

1: Create a final 'skills inventory'

A 'skills inventory' gathers together all the key points you've discovered in steps one to five. To compile your inventory:

✔ List all your skills that are related to management. Don't be put off if your current job title may not say you are 'a manager' – some of your tasks may still be managerial in nature. These tasks can include:

- making and implementing policies;

- carrying out performance reviews;

- hiring and/or firing staff;

- managing projects;

- solving problems;

- managing budgets;

- planning, organizing and presenting work.

✓ List any training you have done – whether as an individual or in a group, and including any informal training. Then list any qualifications you may have been awarded that enable you to teach classes in a particular subject. Include any other professional training courses or seminars you have attended.

✓ List all the times you have prepared reports or manuals, summarized research, conducted studies and so on.

✓ List all your technical skills. Include any specialized knowledge, including any manufacturing, sales, engineering, human resources or other skills that you haven't already mentioned.

✓ List all your interpersonal skills. Although some people find these hard to define, they can often make or break a job application. Interpersonal skills can include:

- being able to communicate clearly and easily with people;

- making things happen;

- helping and instructing more junior staff;

- getting people to agree to compromise if they have different points of view;

- negotiation;

- team building.

✓ Create a category of 'Other Skills' for any that don't fit into the above categories. Often, these skills are something unique that you have to offer, making you potentially more attractive than other candidates applying for the job.

2: Compare the list with your career goals

By now, you should have a good list of your marketable skills. Go back through your list and tick those skills that most closely match your career goals. From these ticked items, choose the 10 that you think are the most marketable. Ask yourself, 'If I were trying to recruit someone for this job, are these the skills I would look for?'

Write a sentence to say how you have actually used each skill from your list of top 10. For example:

- Used conciliation skills to solve a major problem between production and sales.

or

- Conducted quality training in the finance department, leading to a 15 per cent decrease in invoicing errors.

3: Do a reality check

Now, if you can, find someone who is doing the job that you would like to have. Ask him or her to review your list of skills and say if they match this kind of position. If they do not think there is a match, ask what skills you need to gain. Or you could ask what kind of a job would be a better match for someone with your skills.

Alternatively, ask someone close to you to review your skills and to see if you have left anything out. Try to find someone who you know will tell you the truth and offer constructive advice rather than blanket approval – while that's great to hear, it won't be helpful if it's not true.

Step seven:
Get ready to move on

It's time to turn your list of marketable skills into key information in your covering letter and on your CV! The next chapters contain plenty of advice, information and practical help on how to do just that.

TOP TIP

The steps described above will help you to identify the skills that will get you your perfect job. If you plan to change careers, don't worry: many of your skills will be transferable, or you may have skills that you haven't used for some time that could be very attractive in a new position.

Common mistakes

✗ You don't think about your overall career objective

It isn't a waste of time to think about what you've done, what you're doing now and what you want to do next. Working out or just re-examining your career objective will mean that you can home in on the best skills you have or those that you need to acquire, and transfer them to a CV that really does you justice.

✗ You don't bother working out your marketable skills and jump straight into writing your CV

You may think that you already know all your skills, but the exercise outlined in steps one to five always produces some surprising results that can help you market yourself better. Sometimes it even shows you that you may have chosen the wrong job objective. If this is the case, you can shift your career goals towards something that suits you better.

✗ You discount early life experiences

You may believe that it doesn't matter what you did at school or in your first job – for some of us, it may be a long time ago now. However, these early experiences often offer clues to your strongest skills and to where your real ambitions lie.

✗ You're unrealistic about the match between your skills and your career goal

You may want to change from working in IT to a job in human resources, but without any training or experience in the new area, it won't be easy to make the leap. So make sure that you do a reality check before you actually start your job search.

BUSINESS ESSENTIALS

✓ Think about where you are now and where you want to be in a new position.

✓ Work out your career objective.

✓ Be realistic about how your skills match your perfect job.

✓ Be prepared to train or gain new skills in order to fill any gaps.

✓ Take the time to identify your main skills.

✓ Keep the information in your biography short and to the point.

✓ Be confident about your strengths and realistic about your weaknesses.

✓ Look at all sides of your life for your skills: past history, education, leisure activities, life experiences and current work.

✓ Think about those skills that can transfer from job to job easily.

✓ Talk to someone already in a similar job to check that you have appropriate skills, and that it is the job you imagine it to be!

2
Preparing different types of CV

Now that you've spent some time thinking about what you really want to do and the fantastic skills you've got to help you get there, you can focus on transferring all that essential information on to your CV.

There are countless styles of CV, but you need to know how to prepare them. Why? Because every person's career history is different, and you want a CV that puts your career history in the most marketable and attractive light. When you apply for a job, think carefully about which style is most appropriate. A well-written and targeted CV will impress a recruiter much more effectively than a random story of your life.

Your particular job search and career goals are also unique. As you decide which type of CV to prepare, think about whether you plan on staying in the same field or whether you are changing careers. Have you had a fairly standard career trajectory or has your career been less traditional? Is this your first job? Are you aiming for a specific job in a specific company or are you on the lookout for something new and challenging?

All these factors will help you decide which type of CV is most likely to get you the interview that will lead to your perfect job.

Step one:
Choose the right CV for your job search

1: How many types of CV are there?

There is a wide variety of different types, but we will be focusing on the following:

- chronological
- functional
- targeted
- capabilities

A chronological CV is still the most popular type of CV by far, but knowing how to put together the other types will stand you in good stead as you progress through your career and come across different job opportunities. These days, people may have several different careers (not just jobs) in the course of their working lives, so if you're thinking about changing what you do dramatically, a non-traditional CV may suit your needs best.

2: How do the CV types differ?

A *chronological CV* is ideal if you are staying in the same field rather than making a major career change.

This type of CV also works well when you have progressed steadily up a standard career ladder. For example, if you began your career as a junior designer, moved on to become senior designer, and are now hoping to become design manager, this is the CV type for you.

You would also use this kind of CV when you have worked for the same company for most of your career, even though you may have had several different kinds of job within that company.

If you are starting off on your career path, looking for your first or second job, this CV is probably most appropriate to your experience.

A *functional CV* is also a good choice when you are looking for your first professional job or when you are making a fairly major career change.

If you have changed employers frequently, followed a less traditional career path or are concerned that your career history has been a bit patchy, you may be better off with this type of CV, as it focuses primarily on your skills and accomplishments.

Use a *targeted CV* when you are very clear about your job direction and when you need to make an impressive case for a specific job.

It is hard work writing this kind of customized CV, especially if you are applying for several jobs, but it can make you and your abilities stand out from all the others in the pile.

If you are aiming for a specific job or assignment within your current organization, you can use a *capabilities CV*.

Again, you must be willing to take the time to customize your CV for the situation.

3: Should I create a CV for each of these types?

Typically, no. The only exception to this is when you have created one of the standard formats (either a chronological or a functional CV), and a unique opportunity comes up for which one of the customized CVs (either a targeted or a capabilities CV) would be better.

Step two:
Create your CV to fit the situation

There are some basic guidelines to follow when preparing each type of CV.

1: Chronological CV

- Put your name and contact details at the top.

- If you are applying speculatively, state your job search 'objective' clearly.

- Add your employment history. Start with your present or most recent position, and work backwards from there.

- For each position listed, describe your major duties and accomplishments, beginning with an action verb.

- Keep it to the point and stress what you've achieved in each of your roles.

- Keep your career goals in mind as you write and, as you describe your duties and accomplishments, emphasize the ones that are most relevant to your desired job.

- Include your education in a separate section at the bottom of the CV. If you have more than one degree,

they should be listed in reverse chronological order.
List any professional qualifications or training you've
undertaken separately.

> **TOP TIP**
>
> If you've been working for some time, only write in
> detail about your last four or five positions, covering
> the last 10 years or so.
>
> It's fine just to summarize the rest of your career
> history that goes back beyond that.

2: Functional CV

- Put your name and contact details at the top.

- As this type of CV is well suited to people starting
  out in their careers, you may want to include a clear
  job search 'objective'.

- Write between three and five separate paragraphs,
  each of which focuses on a particular skill or
  accomplishment you want to highlight.

- List these 'functional' paragraphs in order of
  importance, with the one most related to your
  career goal at the top.

- Provide a heading for each paragraph.

- Within each functional area, emphasize the most
  relevant accomplishments or results achieved.

- Add in a brief breakdown of your actual work
  experience after the last functional area, giving
  dates (years), employer and job titles only.

- Include your education in a separate section at the bottom of the CV. Again, if you have more than one degree, they should be listed in reverse chronological order.

TOP TIP

Using this CV style means that you can include information about your skills and accomplishments without identifying which employer or situation it was connected to.

This is especially helpful if you've signed a non-disclosure agreement with your current or previous employer, in which you had undertaken not to reveal specific information about a job or project to potential competitors. Non-disclosure agreements are particularly common in tech or research companies, and must be honoured.

BUSINESS ESSENTIALS

3: Targeted CV

- Begin by brainstorming a list of key points. For example, what have you done that is relevant to your target job? Are you proud of what you have achieved? Have you achieved anything in another field that is relevant to your target job? What do you do that demonstrates your ability to work with people?

- Put your name and contact details at the top.

- Think carefully about whether you need to include a job search 'objective' here; as this type of CV is best geared to an application for a specific job, you may not need to include one and could use the space more usefully.

- From your brainstormed list, select between five and eight skills/accomplishments that are most relevant to your target job. Make sure that the statements focus on action and results.

- Briefly describe your actual work experience beneath each skills/accomplishment item, giving dates (years), employer and job titles only.

- Include your education in a separate section at the bottom of the CV, listed in reverse chronological order, as for the other types of CV.

4: Capabilities CV

- To develop a capabilities CV, you first need to learn all you can about the internal job that you are applying for. Then try to come up with between five and eight accomplishments that you have recently achieved that are relevant to this particular job opening.

- Put your name and contact details at the top.

- Think carefully about whether you need to include a job search 'objective' here; as this type of CV is best geared to an application for a specific job, you may not need to include one and could use the space more usefully.

- Next, list your five top accomplishments, focusing on actions taken and results achieved that are relevant to the post you are interested in.

- Write a brief paragraph about any relevant work experience you have had in your current position. If you haven't been at the company for long, you should provide a complete synopsis of your work experience as described for the targeted CV.

- Include your education in a separate section at the bottom of the CV in reverse chronological order.

BUSINESS ESSENTIALS

Common mistakes

✗ **You try to include every skill, capability and accomplishment you have**

It's incredibly tempting to tell a potential employer everything you have ever done to try to impress them. A recruiter or employer will be looking for someone who can get to the point and express him or herself clearly and effectively, though, so remember to keep it simple and focus on those things that are most likely to get you an interview.

✗ **You don't use any particular format**

If you haven't had much experience of writing CVs, you may create one that is a mixture of job listings, skills and accomplishments. This will only confuse your reader.

Rather than leap straight in, work out which type of CV suits your job search or your target vacancy best. Once you've done this, use the sample CVs on pp. 72–79 to help you with the final organization of your material. If you're still concerned about which CV you think will suit you best, it might be worth talking to a career adviser or counsellor. If you are still a student, your school or university careers service should be able to help you for free. If you are working already, you'll probably have to pay for this type of service, and rates can vary quite dramatically so shop around.

✗ You become disheartened

Sales people have learned that you have to take a certain number of rejections before you get a 'Yes'. Finding a job is similar. If you receive a 'No' after making a phone call for an appointment, tell yourself, 'Well, that is one less "No" that I have to hear before I hear a "Yes".'

BUSINESS ESSENTIALS

✓ Think about the job you are applying for so you can choose the most appropriate CV to send.

✓ The most common types of CV are:

- chronological: when you are staying in the same type of work;

- functional: when you are applying for your first job, or for when you have a varied work history;

- targeted: when you know exactly what job you want;

- capabilities: when you want a particular job within your current company.

✓ As far as possible, each time you send your CV out, customize it so it fits in with the job you're applying for.

✓ Don't waffle! Include only relevant information, but take care to explain yourself clearly.

✓ Follow up anything you have said you will do, such as calling to make an appointment.

✓ Don't be put off by rejection. It just means you are one step closer to a 'Yes'!

3
Winning with your CV

> The planning process is over now, and it's time to create the ultimate marketing tool – the CV that will help you get the interview you want.

1: Step one:
Get back to basics

The steps described here are particularly helpful for anyone creating a CV for the first time, but they are just as useful when thinking about how you might update and improve your current CV.

1: Select your CV type

Decide on the best type of CV for your particular background and career goals. Chapter 2 explained the four different types of formats available to you, but in this chapter we'll use a standard chronological CV as an example.

At this stage, also think about the optimum length for your CV. Two pages is fine: it's hard to get across anything useful in just one page, but a CV that is more than three or four pages is far too long and will give the impression that you can't focus or get to the point.

Don't worry if you're a recent graduate – prospective employers still want to know about your achievements. Naturally, they're particularly interested in work experience you've gained, but even musical or sporting achievements will show that you are tenacious and focused.

2: Revisit your career objective statement

Remind yourself about how to create a career objective (pp. 14–15). Make sure your objective still holds true as you compile the different strands of your CV.

Step two:
Order the information on your CV

1: Plan what you want to say

Now's the time to think about the headings you're going to use and the way you're going to order the information on your CV.

The three major categories of information in a typical chronological CV are:

1. contact information

2. career history or work experience

3. education

If you think it's appropriate for your job search, you may also want to include your 'career objective statement' after your contact information.

✔ Begin your CV with information about you and how people can get hold of you if they'd like to invite you for interview. List your name, address, contact phone number and email address. Don't use your existing work email address: it may look as if you're taking advantage of your current employers. (You also run the risk of your current employers finding out about your job search.)

✓ Decide whether your career history or your education is the thing that makes you most marketable. If you are just graduating from university and have not had a lot of professional experience, then you need to highlight your educational achievements first. If, on the other hand, you've been working for some time and have gained skills or experience you want to draw attention to, put your career history first.

Other categories that you might then include in your CV are:

- academic achievements
- fields of study
- continuing education
- professional achievements
- advanced training
- professional affiliations
- computer expertise
- other interests
- references

TOP TIP

Remember that your CV is not a life history. You should include information that is most relevant to your reader, the recruiter, rather than including everything you can possibly think of.

2: Write something for each heading

Listing educational accomplishments is very straightforward and involves giving details of:

- any courses, qualifications or degrees you have completed or are studying for;

- when you completed or are aiming to complete the course(s);

- the name and brief address details of the educational establishment at which you took, or are taking, the course(s).

If you are taking or have completed any professional qualifications, list them in the same way.

Reporting on your professional experience can be much harder, though. To communicate where your expertise lies and to emphasize your achievements, try to begin the statements in this section of your CV with an action verb and include measurable results as far as you can. For example:

> Designed and successfully developed an ISO-9001 program that led to a 19 per cent increase in international sales.

or

> Managed a 300-bed healthcare facility and improved patient satisfaction ratings by 24 per cent over two years.

or

> Liaised with key in-house staff and an international team of freelancers to deliver a complex project on time and £10,000 under budget.

Some people decide not to include information about their other interests (such as sport, travelling, hobbies and so on), but if those interests are important to you, it's no bad thing to include them on the CV – it will give you an opportunity to show a 'fuller' picture of yourself, and also gives the interviewer something to discuss if he or she wants to break the ice or just find out more about you.

TOP TIP

Don't include 'socializing' as one of your other interests if you include them on your CV. You can just about get away with it when applying for a place at university or college, but your CV isn't the place for that type of information!

Similarly, some people choose not to include information about their references on their CV. If you'd rather disclose the contact details of your referees at a later point in the selection process, simply write 'References on request' at the end of your CV as the final heading. If you do want to include your referees on the document, make sure you have their permission to do so before you start sending your CV to recruiters.

Step three:
Write it!

1: Fit the information together

You've decided on the career search you're undertaking, you've worked out your career objective and you've assessed your skills. Now you need to lay out all that experience to best advantage and catch the recruiter's eye.

As a general rule, bear in mind the overall visual impression of your CV – include as much white space as you can so that your CV is attractive and the text uncramped. Also bear in mind the following.

Content

✓ Don't lie about your qualifications or achievements. Remember, a CV is a way to secure an interview rather than a ticket to an instant job offer, so you must be able to back up claims you make on your CV. Very often, you may be given a test as part of your interview (or even an online test before an interview), so if you say you have skills or proficiencies that you won't be able to demonstrate in a test situation, it will be embarrassing for everyone involved. Be proud of the skills that you do have, and make the best use of those. Also, once a person has been appointed to a position, his or her CV goes on the company's file, so there will always be a record of what you said you can do that can be compared with what you really can do.

✓ Customize your CV. There are lots of books and websites that will offer template CVs for every occasion, but be wary of following examples slavishly and remember to bear in mind your target audience at all times.

✓ Explain gaps in your career history. If you went travelling for six months or took a career break to raise your family, say so. You don't need to give lots of detail (particularly if you or a family member have been unwell, say), but wherever possible, stress what you learned in your time out, whether it be new language skills or a talent for organization. Don't be embarrassed to explain if you were made redundant at one point in your career. Many people are affected by redundancy at some point or another and it is rarely a reflection on you, your skills or your capabilities.

Look and feel

✓ Most CVs are submitted via email these days, but if you are asked to send your CV by post, print the document on high-quality white or ivory paper. This will ensure that your CV can be easily read, photocopied or scanned by the recruiter. Also, if hard copies are required, use your own stationery. Don't use headed notepaper or address labels from your current place of work when you are printing out or posting your CV to another company or agency. Just like using your work email as part of your contact details, this will give a strong impression that you are taking advantage of your present employer's facilities.

✓ Take care with the formatting of your CV. Use a 'clean'-looking font that is easy to read (some people prefer a sans serif, such as Arial), and make sure that the type size you use isn't too small. Draw attention to your achievements by using a bold face to highlight positions you've held or qualifications you've gained. Emphasize key points in lists by using bullets.

✓ Make sure you read over your CV once you've finished working on it to check for spelling or grammatical errors – these, above all, will mean your CV ends up in the bin rather than on the right person's desk. It's always a good idea to ask someone else to read over your finished CV, too; he or she may spot something that you've overlooked as you've become so familiar with what you've written.

✓ Try not to rely on computer spellcheckers. While they will pick up on a great many mistakes in spelling and usage, remember that they often won't pick up on words that are spelled correctly but used in the wrong way or in the wrong place. For example, if you write 'there' when you actually mean 'their', the spellchecker might not realize that you've made a mistake.

✓ Follow your own instincts. While a second opinion on your CV is valuable, if you ask 20 people what they think, you'll get 20 (probably different) opinions. In the end, you are the one who needs to feel comfortable with it.

2: Follow up if appropriate

If you have sent a speculative application to a company, it's fine (and in fact shows initiative) for you to get in touch with the person to whom you sent your CV to check that it arrived safely and to see if you can fix an appointment to meet them in person.

If, however, you submitted your CV in response to an advertised vacancy, it's not always advisable to email or telephone to try to arrange an interview. The recruitment process can take a long time, and managers may not respond well to what they might feel is a nagging phone call. Naturally, if you've not heard from a company for some months it's a good idea to contact them then to find out what is happening, but use your common sense and try not to contact them too soon.

3: Keep it up to date

Aim to update your CV at least once a year, even if you are not actually looking for a job. Try to add any new achievements or skills, or clients if you are self-employed, as they occur or you may forget them.

Build an online presence

A CV is a great starting tool in your job search, but creating an online presence, either via a networking website, such as LinkedIn, via social media or blogging, or by creating your own website will also really help.

Networking sites

Registering with a networking site (e.g. LinkedIn) allows you, at a basic level, to create your own profile, where you construct an online CV, listing your achievements, education and experience. But it also helps you to build a network with other professionals, either in your field or in the one that interests you, and create content to connect with others. It also offers opportunities to look for work, as well as professional training, which is sometimes available for free for a limited time.

Social media or blogging

The Internet has democratized access to information. Now, if you want to know about how to get a job in a particular area, you can find out everything you need to know via websites and social media. For particular industries, different social media will be more appropriate. For example, if you want to connect with writers and journalists, you might find following them on Twitter is most helpful. If you're interested in food and photography, then a more visual site like Instagram might be more useful. Take some time to investigate the sites available and find out which one has the most relevant content for your job search. Then start an account(s) that enables you to follow the ideas, people and work that interest you.

If you want to go further, think about setting up your own blog (this is free on platforms such as WordPress) and then sharing that content on the relevant social media platforms. You will start to build a network of people interested in the same areas as you, which may lead to work opportunities and connections.

Create your own

You don't have to be a techie to create a website. There are many hosting companies and platforms where it is possible to build a simple site, often for free, using templates. You can include your photo, CV and any other basic information that might be relevant. Depending on your professional background, you may want to include samples of your work or articles you have written in your specialist field.

If you are seeking a high-tech job or a creative position in the arts or advertising, you might think about purchasing your own domain name and creating a more complex and sophisticated website that could include video, audio, art, photos and whatever else you think will best showcase your skills and abilities to potential employers.

Domain names can be bought very cheaply now, and doing a quick search for sites that offer this service will pull up a whole host of options. Check that you're not being stung for any hidden charges before you buy.

Remember to include your website address on all correspondence, in email signatures, and on your business cards, if you use them.

Common mistakes

✗ You send an old CV because it's all you've got

Don't be tempted to submit an ancient CV when you spot an advert for your dream job out of the blue – if you wrote it five years ago, it won't really represent who you are now and all you've achieved in the meantime. Take some time regularly to update your CV to reflect changes to your job title, your role, any qualifications you've gained or are studying for, or even a pay rise. You'll be less likely to be caught on the hop and you'll be able to react more quickly to new opportunities.

✗ Your CV is too 'busy' and hard to read

You may think that recruiters want as many details as possible about potential candidates who apply for a vacancy, but they really just need to know quickly if you have the basic qualifications and experience for it. You're making their job more difficult if your CV has long sentences, complex paragraphs and too many words on the page.

It's better to have a spacious and easy-to-read two-page CV than a crammed and dense one-page CV. Make your CV visually appealing with lots of indentations, and with lines inserted between sections. Try not to use more than two different fonts and more than three different type sizes – they'll just detract from the content of your CV.

✗ You oversell

Don't be tempted to make what might seem to be boastful or arrogant claims in an attempt to grab others' attention. Instead, back up what you say with measurable results. It is much better to let your achievements speak for themselves.

BUSINESS ESSENTIALS

✔ Think about whether your CV is for a targeted or a speculative career search, as this will affect what you include and how you present it.

✔ Plan your career objective carefully, and make sure you are clear and precise.

✔ Map out your CV in rough first, thinking about the order of the information you will include.

✔ Don't write your life story. Stick to the point and keep your target reader in mind.

✔ Make sure you present your final CV professionally and legibly.

✔ Remember to update your CV regularly, and add any new skills you acquire in case you forget later.

4
Making an impact with your covering letter

When you send your CV to a manager or recruiter to apply for an advertised vacancy or to let him or her know that you are looking for work, you'll normally send a covering letter too. 'Letter' is a bit of a misnomer these days as the vast majority of CVs are submitted by email, but the principles are the same.

If you're applying for an existing vacancy, your covering letter should briefly describe the position you're applying for, where you saw it advertised, why you are particularly qualified for the job, and why you want to work for that specific company. If you're approaching an agency to register your CV as part of your search for a new job, you should describe the type of job you're looking for, the skills you have that would make you an attractive candidate, your current salary, and any preferences you may have in terms of job location.

In all cases, a good covering letter can give a sense of who you are that may not come across in a CV. When you come to write your letter, remember to think about its tone, how you are describing yourself and your skills, and also remember to include the results of any research you've done into the company or field of work you're interested in.

If you sound both interesting and interested in your covering letter, you are much more likely to get noticed, interviewed and employed!

Step one:
Understand why a covering letter is important

The covering letter is the very first thing a recruiter or manager reads. It must grab his or her attention and make him or her want to read your CV and meet you. It is your first chance to stand out from the crowd.

TOP TIP

One way of making an immediate good impression is by addressing your letter to a particular person. Most adverts will give a contact name, but if not, you can ring the company to find out or check on their website.

There are a variety of reasons why you might write a covering letter and send a CV. These include:

- responding to an advertisement;

- following up on meeting someone;

- letting a potential employer or employment agency know that you are available for work.

Other situations may well require a different approach. For example:

- when you send an email to enquire whether there are any job openings. In this email you should ask whom you should send your CV to.

- if you visited an organization in person and filled in a job application.

- when you apply for a job online. If you apply via an agency, you may be asked to fill out a form to accompany your CV. Often, you'll just be asked to give your contact details, but some agencies ask for a brief supporting statement to accompany your CV.

If you are replying to an advertised job vacancy, a covering letter also gives you the opportunity to include details that the advertisement may have asked for but that can't easily be fitted into a CV format. These could include:

- what attracts you to the job;

- current salary;

- desired future salary;

- notice period;

- preferences for geographical location;

- dates you are not available for interview, if relevant (you may want to include these if you are about to go on holiday for a while).

Step two:
Draft the letter

1. Say why you're writing

If you are applying for an existing vacancy, begin your letter by describing the position that interests you and explain clearly why you are writing in the first sentence. You could also say where you saw the vacancy. For example:

> I am very interested in the position of Production Manager as described in your advertisement of 19 September on the Daily Post website.

Alternatively, if you're writing following a recommendation from someone already working at, or known to, the company:

> I have been given your name by Jane Robertson regarding the position in Human Resources.

TOP TIP

You will conduct a more successful job campaign if you combine well-written emails with effective face-to-face, online and phone networking.

2: Show that you're interested

Take time to show that you've done your homework and that you understand what the company does and what its aims are.

✓ Visit the relevant company's website and social media pages and look at any recent news articles, especially its press releases.

✓ Read relevant business newspapers and trade magazines. These will give you a sense of any industry issues facing the company that you are interested in. They may also have particular information about the goals of your target company.

✓ Use LinkedIn and other social media networks to learn as much as you can about the company and the job. If possible, connect via such networks with people who work or have worked at the company, or in similar roles, and see if they will share some of their experiences.

To get across the fact that you've read thoroughly and understood the job advertisement, match the language you use in your letter to the advertisement itself. For example, if the job description mentions 'team leader', refer to that specific job title rather than using the word 'manager'.

TOP TIP

Bookmark relevant websites or articles so that you can find them easily if and when you're asked to an interview for the job.

3: Tell them why they need you

Describe your qualifications early in the letter to grab the interest of the human resources manager or recruiter. Explain how your qualifications will help the organization achieve its goals. For example:

> I understand that your company is planning to relaunch its website to support your sales. In my current position as Director of Internet Sales for Speedy Sales Company, I have helped to increase our market share by 13 per cent in the past year.

Show how you and you alone can help this company deal with any challenges it faces.

4: Suggest an interview

You can do this by saying that you are going to be in the area at a particular time and that you would be available for an interview. Or you can simply say, 'I look forward to discussing how my qualifications can help your organization to be more successful.'

Step three:
Remember the essentials

✓ Keep your letter short and to the point. An effective covering letter is usually only two or three paragraphs long.

✓ Be yourself. CVs are factual records of your experiences and skills. A good covering letter is your chance to show your personality and stand out from the crowd of other applicants as the interview shortlist is drawn up. Keep the letter professional, but don't be afraid to show your enthusiasm, your willingness to work hard and your interest in the position. Potential employers want job applicants who show an interest in them and who seem eager to be a part of their company.

✓ Make sure your covering letter looks professional. Check that there are no grammatical or spelling errors, and read it carefully before you send it off. If possible, ask a friend to check it for you too. Triple-check that you have spelled the name of the person you're writing to correctly.

✓ Use a standard and easily readable font, such as Times New Roman or Arial.

✓ As with your CV, in the rare instance that you are submitting by post, use the highest-quality paper that you can afford. Also, unless you are applying for a particularly creative post, use a plain-coloured paper in ivory or white.

✓ Send any requested hard copies in a large, flat envelope. You may want to send two copies in case the recruiter needs to show your letter and CV to different people, and photocopies or scans will be clearer if the originals have not been folded.

✓ If you are emailing your covering letter and CV, remember to check that you've attached the files before you send the email!

Also, tell the email recipient what type of file you're attaching and be prepared to send it in another format in case they have difficulty opening it.

Common mistakes

✗ You use a covering letter template from a book or website without tailoring it

Reading through examples of covering letters in books can help you to understand what to include, and the layout and tone of this kind of letter. However, you must remember to change the letter to fit your needs. Most managers will have seen hundreds of covering letters and will not want to hear the same old phrases.

Personalize each of your covering letters so that they are targeted at a particular person and company, and so that they represent you and your uniqueness. Some people literally 'fill in the gaps', and write a generic covering letter that they 'customize' by hand-writing the recipient's name and their own signature. Avoid doing this at all costs.

✗ You use the same covering letter for all of your job applications

A covering letter is meant to show that you really want to work for one particular company – taking the time to write a personal, company-specific letter will make all the difference to the impression you give. Using the same covering letter for all your applications also increases the likelihood of you making mistakes when you're tired or in a rush – you may inadvertently mention the wrong company in the body of your letter.

✗ You don't follow up

This is the commonest and most serious mistake. If you said you would phone a recruiter to set up an appointment in your covering letter, you must note the date down and follow it up. Judge the situation carefully, though, and only contact the recruiter if appropriate. See pp. 42–43 for more information.

BUSINESS ESSENTIALS

✔ Tailor your letter to the company and/or person you are applying to.

✔ Do your homework and research the company: the Internet makes this easy, so there's no excuse for not doing this.

✔ If the company's website doesn't have the information, call the company, explain that you are applying for a position, and ask for some promotional literature, such as a catalogue or annual report.

✔ Keep your letter short and to the point.

✔ Show how your experiences and qualifications will help the company directly.

✔ Be polite, enthusiastic and confident in your abilities and skills.

✔ Use good-quality paper (if you're asked to send hard copies) and a clear font.

✔ Proofread everything carefully before emailing it, and ask someone else to read over it as a final check if you can.

✔ If you're replying to an advertised vacancy, check that you've given all the information that the advertisement requested. For example, if the recruiters want to know your current salary and notice period, make sure you've mentioned them.

5
Researching the job market

A great CV and covering letter are key parts of your job search, but to use them to their best effect you need to collect together different types of information as well.

To find the right job and present yourself in the best possible light at interview, you'll need to research industry trends and find out as much as you can about the companies you want to work for.

Keep the following questions in mind as you start your search:

- Where can I find extensive and accurate information about the companies I am interested in?

- What kind of information do I want to know about each of these companies that will help me to write a covering letter that gets me noticed and to perform well at interview?

- What do I need to know about the industry I want to work in that will help me to ask and answer intelligent questions?

- What is the most efficient way I can find and save this information?

Step one:
Do the research

1 Start broadly: research industry trends

In the early stages of your research, you should begin by researching industry trends.

In a nutshell, you need to look out for:

- major growth areas;

- major and up-and-coming players;

- key challenges, opportunities or potential problems for a given industry.

If you are not sure which industry you want to work in, there are several good references and reports on attractive jobs and desirable companies. For example, look at the *Financial Times* website (www .ft.com/companies), which provides well-organized information about trends in various business sectors. The *Economist* website contains extensive articles on business worldwide (https://www.economist.com/ business). One of the most popular guides to company information is the Kompass Register (www.kompass .co.uk). Look also at the websites of the top business schools – these give guidance on where to go and which directories to look at.

TOP TIP

Researching the job market thoroughly will give you a clear idea of what kind of work attracts you. The information you gather will help you design a more effective CV and write an intelligent covering letter.

Step two:
Go from a macro to a micro level

1: Research your chosen companies

The next step is to narrow your research by gathering information about the companies you would like to work for. Aim to find out:

- the size of the organization (sales, profits, market share, numbers of employees);

- its mission statement;

- the company's strong and weak points;

- its key partners;

- its key competitors;

- information about the organizational culture;

- how the company is organized;

- its key strategic challenges;

- the subject of recent press releases.

The vast majority of companies are online these days (and, if they're not, finding out why not might be a question to ask at the interview) so it's relatively easy to get your hands on all this information. Once you have found an organization that you are interested in, get hold of a copy of their annual report from their website. Download it from their site or phone them and ask them to send you a copy.

Also, use social media and networking sites like LinkedIn to learn as much as you can about the company, the sort of culture they have and the type of opportunities they offer.

TOP TIP

Read annual reports from back to front: the important information, such as the facts and figures on how the company's really doing, will be at the back. The glossy PR pages are at the front.

2: Speak to current employees

Once upon a time the only way to talk to someone at a company that interested you would be if you had a direct connection with it, via family, friends or location. The Internet has made it possible to do this from the other side of the globe, knowing no one, if necessary. Use social media and networking sites (e.g. LinkedIn, MeetUp, Xing) to find people who work at the company, tell them you are interested in working at the same place, and ask them if they'd be happy to have a quick chat over email or social media.

Also, get in the habit of telling everyone you know what sort of work and/or opportunity you are looking for, and ask them if they can help. It's really important in a job search to seek out any connection you can find and it's often surprising how easy it can be to have a chat with someone helpful. Be prepared, of course, to do the same for them when necessary!

TOP TIP

If you can't get to know someone who works at your target company, see if your local chamber of commerce can help (www.britishchambers.org.uk).

Step three:
Think about the job you want

1: Research information about a specific job

When you are looking for a specific job in a specific company you will need to ask:

- What qualifications are needed?

- What would my tasks and responsibilities be?

- What is the typical salary for a job like this?

Most of these questions will be answered in your interview, but if you can gather information ahead of time, you will be better prepared for writing your covering letter and your CV, and for your interview. If the job has been advertised, then the tasks and responsibilities will have been listed. If you know for sure that there is a job opening, ask the company to send you a copy of the job description.

Match the time you spend on research to the position. If you are seeking a very high-level executive position in the industry you already work in, you may already know most of the information listed above. If you are seeking a high-level position in a new industry, you may need to spend several weeks on your job market research. If you are seeking a specialized position, you may not need to know as much about industry trends, but you should do several days' research on your chosen organizations.

TOP TIP

Spend time researching industry trends to help you decide whether you want to stay in your current field or whether you'd like to move to something entirely new. If the trends show that you are in a declining industry, it may be time for a change. Also, when you have an interview, your research will help you to ask informed questions.

Step four:
Make the most of everything available

Job alerts

Many recruitment agencies or career-related websites offer an online service to both job hunters and companies trying to fill a vacancy. For job hunters, registering your CV online is a quick and easy process, and means that should an interesting vacancy arise, you can ask the agency to submit your CV quickly.

In addition, take advantage of email job alerts, whereby agencies or career websites email you when a job that meets your specifications comes on the market. This is another quick and easy way to keep on top of job opportunities in your particular market and it will also give you an idea of which companies are expanding or starting up.

TOP TIP

If you do register for email alerts, don't register your current work email address. Use your personal email.

Network

Networking is one of the best ways of getting a new job and finding out about potential openings. The Internet has revolutionized the way that people can keep in touch with each other, and one of the simplest ways to use it for networking is to email people on your contact list. You can ask them about industry trends, potential job openings or for specific contacts within an organization. Other ways of networking on the Web include:

- social media and networking sites. Sites such as LinkedIn and Facebook are just two popular sites that allow you to get in touch with prospective employers or contacts.

- blogs. If you have a blog and a good amount of regular visitors, you could flag up your job search there (but be aware that you do run the risk of your present employer finding out).

As with all other types of networking, though, remember to:

- thank people for their time and help when they get back to you;

- offer your help to other people as much as you possibly can;

- be patient.

Step five:
Be organized

Create your own database of organizations you are targeting, and keep track of information you have gathered about each. Record any job-search actions you take for each organization, such as dates of letters and CVs you have sent, what form of CV you used, dates of phone calls, and whom you spoke to and what was said.

Common mistakes

✗ Your research is patchy

If you don't thoroughly research the industry, the company and the job, gaps in your knowledge may jeopardize your chances at an interview. If you can demonstrate that you have done your homework, you will stand out from the crowd and will have a better chance of being offered the job.

✗ You do so much research that you can't keep track of it all

Create files for each of the industries and companies that you are researching. Organize the information so that you can find what you need quickly – this is especially important when you are preparing for an interview. You could make a set of index cards listing key points that you want to remember, or use a notes function in your phone. Look at these when you get a spare minute to help you learn and remember important information.

BUSINESS ESSENTIALS

✓ For your chosen industry, find out the major growth areas, the major players and the major challenges and problems.

✓ Take the time to find business reference guides and publications online.

✓ Keep your research broad at first, then narrow it down to a few companies you would like to work for. Once you've done that, find out all you can about one chosen company.

✓ Network with everyone you know and online. Speak to existing employees if you can about the company culture, competitors and any challenges the company faces.

✓ Organize all the information you have gathered so that you can find it easily.

✓ Match the time you spend on research to the position you are aiming for.

✓ List what you'd like to know about a specific job ahead of the interview.

6
Choosing the right first job

If you've been preparing your CV for the first time, this chapter aims to give you some help when it comes to finding the right start to your career.

Although people change jobs and indeed career directions frequently these days, it's still important to take care when you choose your first job. Sometimes it can be difficult to know whether you're aiming too low, too high or at the wrong jobs for the wrong reasons. As you start out on your job hunt, think about:

- What kind of a career have you prepared yourself for?

- Are you financially able to hold out for the best job?

- How prepared are you to launch a professional job campaign?

Why is my first job so important?

Nowadays, people very rarely work for one company for the entirety of their working life; in fact, the average person works for 12 or more companies in their lifetime.

When you are looking for your second job, employers will base their evaluation of you on your existing job title and by the reputation of the company where you are working. It is sometimes difficult to go from a low-level position at an unknown organization into a much higher-level position in a well-known organization. On the other hand, it is much easier to go from a good professional position at a well-known company into a better professional position at an even more successful organization. All in all, then, a good first job can often make it easier for you to climb the ladder in your chosen field.

What if I want to work in a non-profit organization?

It doesn't matter: your first job is still important. There is a hierarchy in the voluntary sector in terms of prestige, power, status and success, just as there is in the private sector.

This hierarchy may not influence career choices so heavily, but it still has an effect. Ideally, you are better off establishing your career by working for a well-known and successful voluntary organization than by working for a relatively unknown and unconnected organization. If you truly want to have a positive impact on the world (which is most people's motivation for working in a voluntary organization), you are probably better off if you can do that in an organization with resources and clout.

What key question should I be asking myself?

The million-dollar question is: 'Do I want to be a specialist or a generalist?' If you have chosen a particular field to pursue (such as biology, engineering, finance, music or nursing) that you are really passionate about, then you are probably a specialist. If, on the other hand, you are interested in eventually becoming an organizational leader or an entrepreneur, you are probably more of a generalist. As a specialist, you would want to choose a first job that allows you in time to progress further in your field. As a generalist, you would want to choose a first job that will offer you opportunities to learn more about other fields, and to develop your leadership abilities.

Step one:
Write a 'work purpose statement'

The following useful exercise is adapted from a classic job-seeking guide, *Zen and the Art of Making a Living* by Laurence G. Boldt (Penguin, 1999):

Complete each of the following sentences:

- The way I want to contribute is . . .

- The people I want to serve are . . .

- The scale I want to work at is . . . (for example, individual, community, national, global)

Now combine these sentences into one statement about your work purpose that includes who you want to serve, the way you want to serve them and the scope of the impact you want to make.

Step two:
Explore

1: Think about potential career roles

Make a list of at least 10 different career roles that would be compatible with your 'work purpose statement'. Now select the three that are most interesting to you.

2: Learn about the lifestyle associated with each of these career roles

Use online research and personal contacts (if possible) to get a better understanding of what it would be like to work in each of these potential career roles. Find out what a typical day is like for someone who does that job so you get a realistic picture.

Step three:
Assess your financial situation and your timescale

Work out how long you have to find your first job. If you don't have the financial support to wait for the 'perfect' first job, then decide on your minimum criteria for accepting a position. These criteria could be related to finance, working conditions or geographic location, for example. At the very least, if you are accepting a job that does not fit your 'work purpose statement', then be sure that it gives you the time and opportunity to keep looking for a better position.

Step four:
Start applying

Follow the steps outlined in chapters one to five to find out how to research the job market and create a professional CV and covering letter.

Common mistakes

✗ You choose a career that someone else thinks you should pursue

All too often, people choose a career path that someone else, such as a parent, teacher or lecturer, thinks is right for them. Often, family pressures come into play. If your grandmother and mother were both doctors, you may be expected to follow them in their chosen career path. Resist this pressure if you can, as it doesn't take into account your gifts and talents. If you want to do something else entirely, keep plugging away until you find the right job for you.

✗ You take a job just because it pays well

If you are lucky enough to be offered several alternatives when you are looking for your first job, it is tempting to take the one with the best salary. When you are starting your career, this is what seems to make the most sense but it is short-term thinking. If the job does not fit your personality or your sense of purpose in life, you will either be looking for another job very quickly, or you will stay and be miserable. It's much better to take a long-term view when you accept your first job. Ask yourself how the job will help you develop your skills and achieve your ultimate work goals.

✗ You jump at the first offer

It's understandable that people take the first offer they get even if they've applied for several jobs, especially if money is tight and they're itching to move on and start the next part of their life. It is, however, often a mistake.

If you do get an offer but you're not sure about accepting it, don't be afraid to ask (politely!) for a little time to think over the job offer thoroughly. Make sure you thank the employer for their offer, give them a date (say two or three days hence) when you'll get back to them, and stick to it. If you eagerly accept a position without taking a little bit of cooling-off time, you may be jumping into something when you haven't considered some of the possible pitfalls.

✗ You go to work for a family member or a friend because that's the easiest thing to do

Everybody expects you to join the family business. Or your parents encourage a family friend to take you on. It might seem like an easy solution to finding your first job, but doing this, unless it's what you really want, means abdicating all responsibility for yourself and putting the direction of your life and career in someone else's hands. It may be that one of these opportunities is the perfect one for you, in which case, great. Do take time to analyze and follow the steps above, though, so that you know you are making a rational and informed decision.

✗ You avoid trying to find the kind of work you would really love because people tell you that the job market is bad or it's not practical

It is amazing what you can do if you are determined to make your dream come true. You can be incredibly creative and resourceful. It may be that you will have to work harder and take a little longer to move into the career you would really love to have, but it will be worth it in the long run.

BUSINESS ESSENTIALS

✓ Decide whether you want to be a specialist or a generalist.

✓ Write a 'work purpose statement'.

✓ Think about several potential careers and their associated lifestyles.

✓ Assess your financial situation.

✓ Don't be hasty to accept a job offer. Take time to come to a decision and weigh up all the advantages and disadvantages of the position.

7
Example functional CV

CHRIS O'NEILL
18 My Road
Woking
Surrey
WO20 1XX
email: o_neill@emailaddress.com

A self-motivated and hardworking sales executive with a wide variety of sales experience.

An effective communicator and enthusiastic team-worker with a proven track record, I am looking for a new challenge in a position where my previous experience, sales and communication skills can be successfully put to use.

RESPONSIBLE

I am now responsible for 10 major accounts within a busy sales environment. Although we are operating within an extremely competitive market, my team has consistently achieved and outperformed company sales targets.

Since my arrival, we have grown sales turnover year on year by an average of 30 per cent. I have instigated a policy of regularly following up on lapsed accounts, which has had a success rate of 4 out of 10 customers returning to us after our telephone call.

HARD-WORKING

In each job I have done I have continued willingly to take on more responsibility and to evolve within my role.

I can claim credit for a marked improvement in customer service. In a recent customer satisfaction survey, our ratings were up from an average of 6/10 before I arrived to an average of 8/10.

I have been involved in organizing twice-yearly sales conferences to improve communication between the sales force and other company employees, as well as to enhance relations with major customers.

COMMUNICATOR

Throughout my career, I have effectively liaised with customers across a broad range of business sectors.

I have prepared and presented quarterly and annual projections and budgets.

The activities that I do in my spare time, especially football and acting, are proof of my communication skills.

TEAM PLAYER

I have been responsible for both initiating and organizing several training and morale-building days for the sales force.

As captain of a local football team, I organized training, matches and socials. Under my guidance, the team won more games than they lost during the season – for the first time ever!

I am a member of the Woking Amateur Dramatics Society. With so many busy members, it is quite a feat of organization and teamwork to produce such enjoyable twice-yearly events.

Employment

2017–present Senior Accounts Manager
2015–2017 Accounts Manager
2013–2015 Senior Sales Assistant
2012–2013 Sales Assistant
2011–2012 Administrative Assistant

Training

General IT, including specific training in Excel, Word, PowerPoint

Presentation Skills, Negotiation Skills, Effective Time Management, Teamworking

First Aid

Qualifications and Education

2:2 BA (Hons), Business Studies from University of East Anglia

A-Levels: Business Studies (B), Politics (B), Chemistry (C)

GCSEs: 1 A, 7 Bs, 1 C

Interests

Football, cinema, golf, amateur dramatics and reading.

8
Example speculative chronological CV

Josephine Catterall
5a A Street,
London,
SE30 1YY
email: jfcatterall@emailaddress.com

Objective

To become a HR generalist manager with a leadership
role within a blue-chip environment. I am looking
for a challenging position that will involve managing
resourcing, development and employee relations issues
in the United Kingdom or internationally.

Employment history

*Nov 2017–present HR Organizational Development
Advisor (Latin America), GP International Trading and
Shipping Company Ltd*

Duties

To identify and solve organizational effectiveness problems within GP International and to establish close working relationships with both clients and a network of change experts. This provides advice that will increase the effectiveness of the client's organization and at the same time produce alignment with the main elements of the Latin America cultural change plan.

Achievements

Contributed to the formulation and implementation of the Latin America cultural change plan, especially in areas related to organization design and effectiveness.

Co-ordinated learning activities with a strong link to changing culture or related to collective and organizational development, such as: change management programme, coaching for performance and creating winning teams.

Jan 2016–Oct 2017 Human Resources Policy Adviser, GP International Trading and Shipping Company Ltd

Duties

To provide professional advice on all HR policy matters, including reward and recognition, employee relations, development and resourcing, and to develop UK policy and implement policy changes within the business.

Achievements

Developed an equal opportunities policy and good practice guidance framework for GP companies in the UK, which has enhanced its legislative compliance and understanding amongst staff and management.

Revised the career break policy in conjunction with the policy committee.

Advised HR colleagues on several employee relations issues, including providing employment law advice on disciplinary, grievance and poor-performance issues.

May 2013–Dec 2015 Human Resources Adviser, GP International Trading and Shipping Company Ltd

Duties

To provide front-line, operational advice to three distinct entities of the Global Businesses group: Marine Products, Shipping and Aviation.

Achievements

Coached line managers on how to manage disciplinary, flexible working arrangements, career break and poor-performance processes.

Ran several internal and external recruitment processes through all stages, from advert design and placement to candidate selection.

Designed and delivered a Data Protection Act workshop for the HR department.

Sept 2011–May 2013 Human Resources Business Partner, GP U.K. Exploration and Production

Duties

Provided business-focused advice on a range of issues, including the four main areas of HR (reward, development, employee relations and resourcing) and specifically helped to manage a large-scale redundancy exercise.

Achievements

Part of an HR team responsible for delivering approximately 100 position reductions as part of a cost-reduction exercise.

Acted as staff consultative committee HR representative and secretary – delivered negotiating skills training and team-building workshops to staff reps to improve the quality of their participation.

Education

2010–2011 Postgraduate Diploma in French, McGill University, Montreal, Canada

2007–2010 BA (Hons) Experimental Psychology, University of Bristol

2005–2007 A Levels: Biology (A), French (A), German (B), St Stephen's School, Ely, Cambs

Professional qualifications

2015–2017 MSc in Employee Relations, University of Westminster, London

2013–2014 Graduate of the Chartered Institute of Personnel and Development

Where to find more help

Online

Universities, recruitment agencies and networking sites all offer constantly updated information on how to write a CV and what to include (the latter changes frequently) so be sure to find a few favourites and follow their tips.

For those starting out

What Color Is Your Parachute? 2021: Your Guide to a Lifetime of Meaningful Work and Career Success

Richard Nelson Bolles
Berkley Publishing Corporation: US; revised edition, 2020

Revised and updated annually, this edition of the classic and highly rated job-hunting reference guide works in conjunction with its dedicated website.

The book covers the whole job-hunting gamut, including the alternative job-hunting approach, dealing with rejection, interviews, negotiating a salary and choosing a career counsellor.

For those further along in their career

Pivot: The Only Move That Matters is Your Next One

Jenny Blake

Portfolio: London, 2016

Blake used to work in training and development at Google and now runs her own career coaching and consultancy business. Her book considers change as the essential factor in any career and helps you identify what your skills are and where you want to use them next.

Index

Making an impact in interviews

Now that you've got the perfect CV, here's a sample chapter from *Get That Job: Interviews* – your complete guide to making a fantastic first impression and succeeding in your job search.

Congratulations! You've cleared the first hurdle in your job search with a great CV and covering letter, and have been invited for an interview – you've already found some way to stand out from the crowd. Now you need to build on this success. As you prepare yourself mentally and emotionally for your interview, keep these questions in mind:

- Why do you think you are the best person for the job?

- What is it about this job that attracts you?

- What is it about this organization that has made you apply for the position?

- Who will interview you and what do you know about them?

- What is the appropriate dress and/or image for this organization?

Step one:
Do your homework

Review your CV or application form

✓ Remind yourself thoroughly of all the information on your CV or application form. Think about what questions you might be asked based on your education or work history.

Questions that might be difficult to answer include, 'Why did you choose to study this subject?', 'Why did you leave your last job?' or 'Why did you have a period of unemployment?' Write notes about what you are going to say and practise your answers.

Research the organization

Finding out as much as you can about the company you are visiting will not only help you decide if it is the sort of organization you would like to work for, but may also give you some ideas for questions to ask the interviewer. If you find an opportunity to show that you have done your research, this will signal to the interviewer that you are enthusiastic about the job, as well as knowledgeable about the market.

✓ Look at the company's website and social media feeds, focusing on the annual report, news, press releases and biographies. This will give you a feel for the organization – its key values, its success factor and its people.

✓ Research current factors that might affect the organization, such as industry trends, competitive issues, strategic direction and particular challenges or opportunities.

Step two:
Decide what you want to get from the interview

✓ Identify the key points you want to make about your strengths and skills. When you prepared your CV, you listed the key strengths and skills that you thought an employer would be looking for. Revisit that list, choose a skill and think of a recent situation you have been in that will demonstrate that strength or skill to an interviewer. If possible, include any concrete results achieved due to that particular strength or skill.

TOP TIP

It is important to focus on the positive in your answers, even when you have been asked to talk about a difficult situation or your weaknesses. That way, you will come across as someone who rises to a challenge and looks for opportunities to improve and develop.

✓ Prepare a mental list of questions you would like to ask the interviewer(s). Remember that you are also interviewing the organization, so put together a list of questions that will help you decide whether or not this job is a good fit for your personality and your career goals. In addition, well-thought-out and pertinent questions will help to demonstrate your interest in the company and your enthusiasm for the post.

TOP TIP

Avoid asking questions about benefits and salary at a first interview, unless the interviewer brings them up. Get the offer first, then talk about money! For advice on negotiating a good benefits package, see Chapter 14.

Step three:
Prepare yourself mentally

Many people, from athletes to salespeople, prepare themselves for challenging situations by mentally picturing a successful result – a method that can also be used before attending an interview.

✓ Before the interview, imagine yourself being professional, interesting and enthusiastic in your interview. Also imagine yourself leaving the interview with a good feeling about how you did. This will put you in a positive frame of mind and help you to be at your very best in the interview.

✓ Arrive 15 or 20 minutes early so that you can take some time to relax after your journey. Go and freshen up to help you feel more comfortable and confident. Drink some water, flick through company magazines if they are available. Try to get a feel for the atmosphere, as this will help you to decide if it's the sort of place you can see yourself being happy working in. It will also give you an idea of what to expect in the interview, and the sort of candidate the interviewers will be looking for.

✓ Ask a friend or family member to role-play the interview with you. School and university career counsellors and career coaches will also do this. Give this person a list of questions that you think you might be asked. Role-play the interview and ask for the other person's feedback. Film it if you can so that you can watch your body language.

Typical interview questions

Prepare answers to these standard questions that interviewers often ask:

- Tell me a little bit about yourself.

- Where do you see your career five years from now?

- What are you most proud of in your career?

- What is your greatest strength?

- What is your biggest weakness?

- Describe a difficult situation and how you handled it.

- Can you tell me about a time when you had to motivate a team?

If you are a recent graduate be prepared to answer questions like these:

- Why did you choose your degree subject?

- How will your studies relate to your work?

- What have you enjoyed most at university?

TOP TIP

When asked to tell the interviewer a bit about yourself, they don't want a life history. The interviewer is using this as an ice-breaker so give a brief overview of yourself, including a short history of recent employment.

Step four:
Create a positive impression during interview

✓ Be punctual. Better still, be early to give yourself some preparation and relaxation time. If you're not sure of the location of the company, you might want to do a practice run of the journey so you can be sure to leave yourself enough time.

✓ Be enthusiastic. Know why you are interested in this job and make sure you show your interest. Interviewees who are excited about the organization get job offers! Don't say that you are interested in the job because it pays well. Instead, be ready to talk about what you can offer the company, how the position will expand your skills, and why this kind of work would be satisfying and meaningful to you. Don't overdo it, though, as this may come across as insincere or overconfident.

✓ Be honest. The overall impression you are trying to create is of an enthusiastic, professional, positive and sincere person. These things will come across from the word go, if you follow the basic rules of giving a firm handshake, a friendly smile and maintaining good eye contact throughout the interview. Never lie in the interview or attempt to blag your way through difficult questions. Good preparation should ensure that you don't have to resort to this. Speak clearly and respectfully. Swearing and flirting are definite no-nos.

✓ Practise 'image management'. It is important to look good and to sound professional in an interview. You should feel comfortable in what you wear, but it is better to turn up 'too smart' than 'too casual'. People will take you seriously if you dress respectably. If you are applying for jobs in media or the arts, a suit may not be necessary, but dressing smartly will always give the impression that you care about getting this job.

TOP TIP

It's always a good idea to take some anti-perspirant with you to an interview, as when people are nervous they tend to sweat. You may also find yourself a bit hot and dishevelled if you had to rush to get to the interview in good time (although if you have prepared your journey well, this shouldn't happen!). Make sure you have time to freshen up before the interview. This will help your confidence, and spare the interviewers a sweaty handshake or, worse still, a bad odour when you enter the room. On the other hand, don't go overboard on the perfume or aftershave – that would count as a bad odour, too.

✔ Wherever possible, back up your responses to questions with evidence-based replies. For example, if an interviewer asks you how you manage conflict within a team, give a brief general response and then focus on a specific example of how you have done this in the past. Illustrating your answers with real examples gives you the opportunity to focus on your personal contribution, and will be more impressive than giving a vague, hypothetical reply.

TOP TIP

Remember that the interview is a two-way process – not only is the organization trying to decide on the best person for the job, you are also trying to decide on the best organization to work for and the best job and career choice for you.

Common mistakes

✗ You misread the culture or the personality of the person interviewing you

People tend to underestimate the level of formality and professionalism required in an interview. Some interviewers even create a more social than professional situation to catch you off-guard. If you find yourself in an interview with a more casual approach than is appropriate, change your behaviour as soon as you notice. The interviewers are more likely to remember your behaviour at the end of the interview than at the beginning. On the other hand, if the environment or the interviewer is more formal than you realized, don't worry. You are expected to look and act in a highly professional and formal way in an interview. Use your instincts to judge how much you need to change your behaviour to show that you would fit into the company culture.

✗ You use humour inappropriately

To make a situation less tense, people sometimes use humour to lighten the mood. But if you have said something you think is funny and received a negative reaction, it's best not to call attention to the situation by apologizing. Try to act as if nothing happened and go back to behaving professionally. Whatever you do, don't follow inappropriate humour with more humour.

✗ You didn't do your homework

You get to the interview and realize that you really know nothing about this organization. What do you do? Well, hopefully, you arrived early and have some time in reception. Take the opportunity to do some research on your phone. Often, booklets and leaflets found in receptions provide quite a bit of information about the company, its industry, its products and services. Look at them, look around, and learn everything you can. Talk to the receptionist and ask them questions that may be helpful to you in the interview. It is possible to learn quite a bit about the organization on the fly, but nothing works better than doing your homework.

✗ You criticize your current or former employer

Avoid this at all costs. It gives the interview a very negative feeling, and will leave the interviewer wondering if you would criticize this organization when you left. This kind of criticism usually happens when someone is asked why they are leaving (or have left) their last position. The best way to answer this is to talk about the future rather than the past, and to show your keenness to take on challenging career opportunities.

BUSINESS ESSENTIALS

✓ Be completely familiar with everything on your CV, and be prepared to answer any difficult questions on your education and/or work history.

✓ Do your homework on the company before you go for your interview.

✓ Fix your key skills and strengths in your mind, so that you can make sure you mention them when given appropriate opportunities.

✓ Prepare honest and clear answers to standard interview questions.

✓ Remember that you are also interviewing the organization, so have a list of questions for the interviewer ready.

✓ Ask a friend or family member to role-play the interview with you, and ask for their feedback.

✓ Arrive early at the interview to give yourself time to relax, freshen up, absorb the atmosphere and even spend time visualizing a successful result.

✓ Be enthusiastic in the interview and excited about the job.

✓ Don't talk about benefits and salary in a first interview, unless the interviewer brings them up.

✓ If you feel you have misread the level of formality required, change your behaviour appropriately as soon as you notice.

✔ If you use humour inappropriately, act as if nothing has happened and get back on track. Don't make another joke to cover it up!

✔ Don't ever criticize your current or former employer. Talk about the future instead.

If you prepare well for an interview by knowing your CV, listing likely questions and responses, researching the company and the people, role-playing the interview and dressing appropriately, you will arrive at the interview feeling confident and enthusiastic. This confidence will help you make the best impression that you can so you may come away feeling proud of yourself for having done your very best – whatever the outcome.

Get That Job: Interviews (9781472993298) is published by Bloomsbury Business and is part of the *Business Essentials* series. Available from all good bookshops or at www.bloomsbury.com

BUSINESS ESSENTIALS